turning

turning

words heard from within

Claire Blatchford

Lindisfarne Books

© 1994, 2001 Claire Blatchford

Published by Lindisfarne Books
  PO Box 799, Great Barrington, MA 01230
  www.lindisfarne.org

Library of Congress Cataloging-in-Publication Data

Blatchford, Claire H.
  Turning: words heard from within/by
  Claire Blatchford.
    p.cm.
Originally published: Hudson, NY:
  Anthroposophic Press, c1994. With new introd.
  Includes index.
  ISBN 0-9701097-7-6
Anthroposophy. 2. Spiritual life. I. Title.

  BP596.S66 T87 2001
  299'.935
  dc21
  2001016510

10 9 8 7 6 5 4 3 2

CONTENTS

Mary stood weeping outside the tomb, and as she wept she stooped to look into the tomb, and she saw two angels in white, sitting where the body of Jesus had lain, one at the head and one at the feet. They said to her, "Woman, why are you weeping?"

She said to them, "Because they have taken my Lord, and I do not know where they have laid him."

Saying this, she turned round and saw Jesus standing, but she did not know it was Jesus.

Jesus said to her, "Why are you weeping? Whom do you seek?"

Supposing him to be the gardener, she said to him, "Sir, if you have carried him away, tell me where you have laid him, and I will take him away."

Jesus said to her, "Mary."

She turned and said to him in Hebrew, "Master."

The Gospel of St. John 20:1116

AUTHOR'S INTRODUCTION
to the Second Edition

It is wonderful and even startling to know that what has come out of one's own still and holy moments of prayer and listening is of help to others. During the six years since *Turning* was first published, I have heard stories of readers opening the book to "exactly what I needed to hear." What has really given me goosebumps, however, are the accounts of those who were encouraged by the words I received to ask the Divine world for help and guidance—and then knew, without a doubt, that they had received it.

For *Turning* is, above all, about turning, not to this or that page, or to this or that author, teacher, or method, but to the One who is right here, right now, within, beside, and all around, waiting to be acknowledged and invited into our lives.

> "I long for people to look at me directly,
>   not through books or other people.
>   Many are fearful;
>   they think they aren't good enough to seek me directly."

"I am closer than you think.

    You don't have to shoot out into space to connect.

    There's a space between too far out and too close in

    where you can be with me easily and comfortably

     without strain."

The words that make up *Turning* were heard some twenty years ago. The hearing was inward, occurred almost every day at any time no matter where I was or what I was doing, and brought with it a joyous and blessed sense of well-being that can only be described in one way: I felt as though I had found and been found by Love.

The inner hearing of the voice that spoke these words began early one morning quite simply and naturally. I say "simply and naturally" because I now see as I look back that I had been prepared for what was to come.

First, I was prepared by occasional experiences of inner hearing when younger. I lost my hearing overnight at the age of six through mumps and was compelled to learn to listen in every way I could. As I listened to others, primarily through my eyes, I sensed that I lived in two worlds: the world "in here" as well as the world "out there." I could not see the world in here the way I could see the outer world, but I could hear it. I could hear the sounds and the voices of the thoughts and feelings that moved within and through me. Anger was loud and domineering, discouragement whined, happiness sang.

Then there was another voice, a clear, calm authoritative voice that spoke every now and then. This voice could cut right through the unpleasant inner sounds, could bring comfort, and could move me to action in a way nothing else could. What it said was usually quite simple, such as, "You're okay," or "Go help your mother."

I never doubted what I heard when this inner voice spoke, for the words made sense, always helped, and did away with the notion that I was different and cut off because I was deaf. I believed—and I believe this as earnestly now as when I was a child—that this voice is available to all. Deafness just brought it to my attention. Each person's experience of hearing it may, however, be different. For some it may be more of a gut feeling, a knowing, than an actual voice. For others it may manifest as a seeing of inner pictures, as in dreams or waking dreams, rather than words. My understanding of this is that the senses often fuse and become one, seeing becomes hearing, hearing becomes seeing, smelling becomes seeing and hearing, and so on. But, no matter how we may become aware of it, the spiritual world is there and all of us possess the faculties to perceive and connect with it.

Second, I was prepared by a young man I had met in a small publishing enterprise where I had submitted a novel for consideration. I was amazed by the insightful comments he made about my manuscript, and soon we were talking about many more things than writing. Then one afternoon I received a brief note from him in which he said "someone" wanted to meet me. He did not say who wanted to meet me, and I felt no need to ask whom he meant because all of his communications with me had been inspiring and helpful. I just knew when I read the note that I believed in this someone, that this someone was not visible to ordinary human sight, and that I too wanted the meeting to occur.

My reaction was to put all aside, go out, and walk. I walked out into the open until I felt the urge to sit down. It was a lovely quiet early evening in August. There was a tall pine in front of me. As I gazed at it, it seemed to say, "Not I, but Him." I felt myself turn, not outwardly but inwardly, and there was the "someone" beside me. I could not see this being with my physical or inner eyes but, with my whole soul, I knew He was there and had been near throughout my life.

After about an hour I returned home. I felt filled up to over-flowing with wonder and devotion. The next morning I woke early, found a pen and pad and began writing what I heard inwardly. For a little over three years I did this.

In other words, this young man prepared me to be open to the presence of the good, the true, and the beautiful, and to be ready for the unexpected. I believe such preparation can occur in many ways: by meeting or hearing others who have had uplifting experiences, through the reading of the accounts and discoveries of such people, and above all through the hunger in our hearts for "something more."

At the end of the three years the inner words came less and less frequently and then ceased altogether. I was distressed; now I was truly deaf and alone. I prayed for understanding of the situation and when nothing was forthcoming decided the only thing I could do was to express gratitude for the experience. The minute I began to give thanks I knew release from distress and confusion and felt new eagerness to get on with life. I believe that even as I have known times of deep meeting and also times of separateness in close human relationships, there are times of feasting and times of famine in my relationship with the Divine. And the important thing is to hold myself steady in a place of faith and gladness, no matter what the offering is.

One day twelve years later I suddenly felt the urge to look for the journals which sat forgotten in a large box in the back of my closet. I was moved to tears as I read the pages. Mine were tears of joy, not sadness, for I heard the voice again as I read! Faintly at first and then stronger and stronger. I heard it not only agreeing with what had been said earlier, it added new emphasis, warmth, and commentary. And it continued after I finished reading. It was as though my innermost ear of ears had had to fall asleep for awhile in order to wake up a bit more.

The voice suggested that I type up the journal pages and share them with a long time friend and mentor, John F. Gardner. John took them as much to heart as I had. It was he who felt the messages should be gathered together as a book and ordered by theme rather than chronologically. It was he who told me to ask inwardly for the title rather than trying to think one up. And it was he who believed that *Turning* is not meant simply to be read from cover to cover. As he said so well and rightly in his introduction to the first edition:

"We do not always know what we most need to hear, and so on many occasions readers may find themselves well guided if they open this volume at seeming random, having in mind only to take special note of the page and passage on which their glance then falls. Often the "word" to be found there, when given more than passing attention, turns out to be the best advice one could have received at the moment."

Lastly, it was also John who said he believed that the voice speaking through the pages was the voice of Christ. His own wide and searching reading throughout his long life led him to this conclusion. I was astounded. Though I had prayed to God frequently as a child and had composed my own psalms, the out-of-doors, particularly any river or beach by the ocean, was my Bible. I had given little thought to Christ Jesus in my teens except when being confirmed in the Episcopal Church. He was for me, at that time, more of a historical figure than anything else. In my late twenties inspiring books by Mary Fullerson, George Ritchie, Rudolf Steiner, and others came my way, but I still could not perceive how close He is. Then, during the three years when the "someone" was conversing with me, I did not think to ask who was speaking because I felt no single word could encompass all the comfort, the inspiration and even the laughter that the voice offered so freely and abundantly. Yet my heart leapt up with a quick and clear, "Yes!" when John spoke of Christ.

Later, when the voice said my name was not to be on the first edition of *Turning*, for my own protection and because it was important that the words be heard by themselves, I readily agreed. As I was told:

"If the inner ear is attentive in those who read this book, they will hear me and they will begin to find what they need, not only in these words but in their own hearts."

It is my hope that those readers who think of Christ Jesus in a respectful yet distant way will discover a new and deeper friendship with Him. It is also my hope that those readers who recoil at any mention of the name of Christ will now dare to leave all personal beliefs, religious affiliations, and unpleasant memories associated with this name, outside on the steps. Come on in, and dare—if only for a few moments—to listen to what I heard. And then decide if what you have read speaks to you and, more importantly yet, continues to sound in your heart, not necessarily as words but as new hope, new belief, and new gladness.

Christmas 2000

Let me breathe in you

Center your being on me.
All day long return to me;
Do not worry about the world;
Think only on me
And I will draw you into myself.
All fear must go;
Otherwise you will not hear.
Let me breathe in you:
Light and darkness will balance,
You will not fear either.

Know that I love you.

You will know my voice when you hear it.

Accept   your   darkness

Accept your darkness and heaviness,

Do not fight against them alone.
Once you've accepted them as they are,
Recognized your weaknesses,
And opened yourself to me,
Light will flow into you
And darkness will move out.

You are wholly new

Learn to awaken every morning to me
And to meet me in the silence,
Without thoughts of the coming day and what
must be done,
And without the influence of dreams.
You are wholly new: *think that*—
Facing forwards, towards the light,
Like a plant groping up through the ground,
Groping towards the air and the light.
Sense the light coming to meet you,
Bask in the warmth, fill yourself with it,
Leave the past behind in the ground,
Leave behind any hopes or expectations you
    have for the future—
Except that you may be mine
And may know the Father's presence.

When you are newborn
You are born away from all that you were.
Let this feeling, this thought of newbornness
Swell and grow in you.
Let it become a power in you, let it become a
    light
Leading you on, though you know not where.
Trust it, believe it, follow it into each day.
Cease worrying about what you should or
    shouldn't do,
Listen for me—that above all.

Wipe the slate clean

Every day begin again:
Have no remorse,
Nor pride in where you think you might be.
Wipe the slate clean,
Come to me whole and new.
Come to me empty
Yet full of gladness and praise.
Look on each day as a new creation
And you will be new also.
Let there be expectation in you,
Eagerness to see what the day may bring.
Only the old live in the past or the future.
Imagine the day is full of gifts,
Some deserved, some not,
Many, perhaps, what you won't consider "gifts"!
Let your gift to me be yourself,
Willing my will,
Awaiting my word.

Expect nothing,
Desire nothing,
Except to be open
To what Your Father knows
Is truly yours.

Alive to Our Father

How you greet the morning,
How you say good-bye to the day—
Be alive to that,
To every gesture of your soul.
There are points where your gestures are met
     and returned
Like a handshake, or a smile.
Who is at these points?
Our Father.

Enjoy life

Enjoy the life that has been given to you in
    such abundance.
How glad Our Father is when you enjoy what
    He has given you.
Don't you want to give more, and yet more,
When you see those you love enjoying what you
    have given them?

In the center of your being

Be quiet,
Be calm,
Think of me as waiting in the center of your being
Within your heart.
Think of me as a room you can return to
     whenever you are weary.
There are no harsh lights or noises in this room,
Only the clear, steady flame of a candle,
Only harmonious music.
As you rest in me
The room slowly grows larger,
The walls move out and out
And disappear.
Stars, angels,
The sun, the moon,
Clouds, winds,
The faithful plants and beasts
All draw near,

All are with you in me.
So in weariness and confusion you contract
    and breathe in
To the center wherein I wait for you.
When you have rested awhile in me,
Let your soul expand and soar,
Let it breathe out
Borne on currents of faith and hope.

Two morning verses
(To be said aloud when needed)

That which created and daily recreates me
Is out there—
That which is out there,
In the stars, the plants, the animals, in all
    human hearts
Is within me.

First seed, first spring of water, first word,
May you stay clear and strong,
That all which comes from you,
O fountain of the Godhead,
May know how to return to you,
And be strengthened and renewed.
Father, I have been with you.
I thank you for the new strength you have given
    me;
I thank you for the place on this earth in which
    you have put me;

For everything you have placed me with,
For everything in every person,
Regardless of how it affects me in my feelings.

Father, I trust your wisdom for ever and ever.
Fill me with the right thoughts, feelings and
    impulses;
Guide my will so it be Your will.

Every day

Every day is an eternity,
Savour and cherish it.
Every minute is an eternity.
Walk with me in the garden
Of sunlight
Where light beings weave their flowers
And angels sing.
There you will want nothing
But to be in my presence,
Such calm will be in your heart.
All your loves will gather
And flower there.
All your thoughts will become
Birds in the air.

We will sit together by the river
And I will tell you where it goes.
Further than eyes can see,
Beyond the reach of ears,

You will see the colors
Of living waters flowing there.

Do the best you can

Do the best you can every day.
Resolve quite simply with no great ambition,
To be your best self,
To do each task as well as you can,
To give thanks for being alive.
Do not throw up your hands in despair
If you fall short.
Do not dwell on your errors and moments of
    forgetfulness.
When that happens just pick up the thread
    where you left off and go on.

Turn to me

My life on earth—
That is only one aspect of me that you can seek.
Whichever way you turn within your life on
earth
You will find me.
Know that I am also out there in the heavenly
spheres,
Growing and creating
By the laws of those spheres too.
The task of humanity
Is to help bring what is in the heavens down to
earth.

The heavenly beings are at once separate and
within each other;
This is hard for humans in their materialism to
understand.
Think of desire, how the force behind it is
fusion and possession.

In heaven desire is transformed into love,
For in Love all are one.
And yet each being has its own color, form, note.
Humans, too, can know such love on earth:
Pure love, without desire,
Love that places one within the very heartbeat of
    the Father
And makes one whole
As one seldom knows wholeness on earth.

I am at once within you, about you, and every
    where.
However, when you open to pride, greed, desire
    or any other dark force,
You close me out.
You become hardened within yourself,
You sense your incompleteness and panic,
You forget me;
You want more and more,

And are pulled down.
Know that love can dissolve these barriers
    instantly,
Can bear you up again
When you, of your own will, out of your heart,
Turn to me.

Let me in

Try daily to disentangle yourself from all about you.
Feel yourself rising out of your house, out of the
    city, out of the land
Higher and higher.
All the worries you know are becoming smaller and
    smaller—mere specks.
Those you love are far away and yet they are *in* you.

Feel yourself rising through clouds and mist—
Look down, see the oceans
Stretching out all around
Over the surface of the earth.
How tiny, yet precise
Is the outline of the land!
How vast, blue, and mysterious is the water!
What seems like huge sky with stars overhead is
    becoming familar.
The hugeness flows into you

And is not longer huge.
You flow into it
And feel the presence all around of other beings:
The so-called dead, angels, others.
You feel them and long to be in their company,
    to see them;
Yet things in you are still dark and weigh you
    down,
They prevent you from seeing and hearing this
    other world.

You feel less a stranger here
Than on earth;
Yet some part of you is still closed,
Closed tight to the magnificence.
It is like a small, tight, dark, windowless room.

Work to find this room.

You will be surprised at what you can find
Though you think you've come far already.
Bear the light into this room,
Clean out the dead objects,
Let the air in—
Let me in.

Oneness with all

I can be within all at once.
I can speak to all at once.
This is beyond anything you can understand now.
Don't get dizzy thinking about it.
Let the sense of it unfold within,
Slowly, lovingly.
And you will come to feel oneness with all.

Union with me

Every soul can unite with me.
Every soul can marry me,
No matter the sex that soul has chosen to be on
    earth.
Male or female,
Come to me, be made whole.

You will know true purity in union with me,
True innocence.
Give me your joys,
We will give thanks together.
Give me your sorrows,
And the sorrows of others that you feel so deeply,
Let me lift them from you.
Give me your doubts and misgivings,
Your temptations and failings,
That the bond between us may grow strong.

Learn how to keep house with me.
Honor and care for your body,
Honor and care for your soul,
Keep your thoughts and feelings in order.

When I go away
Wait patiently.
Go about your work as usual,
Steady in the faith that I will return,
For I will.
I never abandon those I have wed.

Seek me directly

I long for people to look at me directly,
Not through books or other people.
Many are fearful,
They think they aren't good enough to seek me
directly.

Be not afraid to come to me at *all* times.

The direct approach

There is no subsititue for the direct approach
to me.
Everyone must do it alone,
Not through anyone else.

I am closer than you think

I am closer than you think.
You don't have to shoot out into space to connect.
There's a place between too far out and too close in
Where you can be with me easily and comfortably
    without strain.

It is your doubt that prevents you from hearing
    clearly.

The inner voice

The inner voice is buried deep within.
It speaks when you are entirely attentive to it.
Sometimes it speaks when you least expect it.
When the outer world presses in
And the mind is distracted by the many voices,
Then it is easy to doubt the inner voice.
The inner voice is as real as any outer voice.
Given the chance
To grow loud and clear,
It will guide you safely and surely,
It will tell of wonders and powers
Within.
Allow it to speak through more than a key hole—
Open the door to receive it.
Tend to it
Jealously, lovingly.
Watch your words, your actions, your thoughts,
That the door not be suddenly slammed shut.

I am always speaking to you

Be humble in the knowledge
That I am always speaking to you,
Though you do not always hear me.
Sometimes I speak without words,
Through others,
Through light,
Through dreams,
Through music.
When you can't hear me
Acknowledge your deafness,
Give thanks for it,
Let it sharpen your appetite.

Come at once

When I call you, do not dally;
Leave off what you are doing and come at once.
Great will be the sorrow
Of those left behind,
Because I called and they didn't come.
You know with your own children
How cross you get
When they don't respond.
How much greater will *my* anger be,
When whole nations fail to hear.

Sometimes I will not answer right away because
     you may not be ready,
Or because you need to work a bit for the answer.

Ask from your heart

Great is my joy when you ask from your heart.
Bring me *all* your questions,
No matter how trivial they sound to you.
Listening is but half of a relationship,
Asking is the other half.
Know how I hunger for this dialogue with you!
Can you imagine what it is like to see into hearts
And not be invited to speak with them?

Did you hear?

How does one find me?
By listening.
How does one remember me?
By listening.
How does one escape one's small, petty self?
By listening.
Did you hear that?

Old pains, give them to me

You are not asking me all the time all day
What you are to do.
There is so much of yourself
That you have not handed over to me:
Old experiences, old pains, heavy old thoughts
That lie deep within.
Dig them up
—Don't worry how they smell!—
Give them to me,
That they may become compost for new growth.

Shaped anew

Do not come to a standstill at the realization
That you receive guidance.
Follow it, *believe* it, *love* it.
Then it can shape you.
It is not simply a matter of your taking it,
But of its taking you.
It is the difference between standing on the shore,
Feeling an occasional wave on your foot,
And going *into* the ocean.
That way you will be truly shaped anew.

The bread is my word,

the water is my love

The bread is my word—
Receive it with gladness
And obey.
It will never diminish;
Rather, it will grow greater, stronger, clearer.
Only when you eat
Do you take it into yourself
In every way:
It works upon you,
You receive from it all the nourishment you need,
So is it called bread.

Do not try to understand this with your head
    alone—
Let it live in you.

The water is my love.

As water flows.
So does love flow.
One cannot eat bread alone,
There must be water also.
And one cannot drink water alone,
For the bread brings one into the house of my
    being.
Only there can one take hold
Of that which is given
And make oneself a vessel
Of my will.

Many feel the water,
But few eat of the bread.

Begin now

Begin *now*.
Do not say, "I will begin when . . ."
As though you could overcome your weaknesses
and faults all by yourself.
Bring them to me daily, humbly.
Know that I receive you joyfully, even if you bring
   the same things to me
again and again and again.

How much time you give to me doesn't matter—
What matters is what you bring to this time,
And that you come regularly.

May the spiritual continue to unfold

How meager is your conception of time!
Things are never past and over—
Great things, things of the spirit, that is.
Physical events occur and fall away like discarded
    skins.
Great spiritual events may appear to have happened
    and passed on
But in reality they are reoccuring daily.
I am dying daily and being reborn daily.
Live into this realization,
Ask to be able to perceive it,
That even the spiritual may continue to unfold.

These spiritual events and truths are never known
    once and for all.
You are too small for that.
Rejoice when you see a portion of the truth
But don't cling to it, or imagine that
Because you have seen it, it is the ALL.

Truth is fluid;
The shape you see today may be quite different
    tomorrow.
And yet its origin is the same,
Is One, is in the Father's Word forever.

Daily admit your own ignorance, your nothingness,
Thereby opening yourself
That the truth without
May enter and feed the truth within,
The truth that is at the core of your being.

From deep within and far without

I do not want you to be sealed off from life—
As you go inwards
You must go outwards:
Look for me in both places.
Hold yourself empty,
Pass no judgment;
Then I can come into you
From deep within,
From far without,
And teach you true compassion.

The Cross

Some souls travel straight forward through
    their lives
From one thing to another,
On and on.
I would have you also travel deep down and
    high up.
This way you will find the Cross,
The true center of your being.

Venturing all alone

You cannot grasp hold of me, and keep me,
For I am always changing.
You must change also,
To know me.
So give thanks for your confusion
As you travel through doubt and darkness.

I gave you a taste of my bread.
Now you want more.
First you must leave others behind
And venture all alone
Into the darkness.
No one can make the journey with or for you.
You are searching for me;
Do not rest till you have found me.
Silence, expectancy, a willingness to leave off
    whatever you are
doing and to come—

Those are your companions,
And the cross—carry it high in your moments
of fear and doubt.
You must learn how much greater your light
can be.
That is why I have taken your little bit away for
now.
Search for it
By being open to all people,
By listening with all your being
And silencing your thoughts.
Hold the cross high when in doubt.

I have many ways

You want to be on the Right Way.
I am the way;
Yet I have many ways,
As many ways as there are souls in the world.
Your mind wants to know
If other people's paths
Are like your own.
Restrain your mind
Every time it gets going down this path;
It leads only to discontent.
Restrain your mind,
Yet through appreciation open it to others
That some day it will be able to recognize my light
In *all* ways.

Find your bearings with me

When you make a schedule
You feel secure in it
But perhaps *I* am closed out.
The schedule is of your mind,
Let your mind cease grasping.
You must learn to flow like water.
You must learn to be certain inwardly
When outwardly all appears uncertain.
You must learn to find your bearings with me
Anywhere, any time.
You must learn how each minute is precious
    and has its message.
Learn by praising me whenever you feel uncertain,
    insecure, anxious.
Let praise loosen, open, and become your very breath

From within outwards

You are waiting for outer events
To determine the course of your inner life.
You've got it backwards.
Live from within, from your connection with me,
Outwards.
Then outer events will come *to* you,
Will surprise you in wonderful ways.

True security

You're worried about the future?
Good!
Learn to live with what you think of as insecurity,
Feeling the bottom
Might be kicked out any minute.
Don't take Our Father's gifts for granted,
Learn all over again to give thanks for life.
Learn the source of true security
In me.

The deepest longing

Is not every person's deepest longing,
To serve the Lord and know that he is loved?
When stripped of their clothes
All ambitions, all strivings
Reveal this truth,
Though man himself may not know it.

Do not allow disappointment or discouragement
    to cloud your vision
Ever!
Discouragement is of the devil!

Do not let the earth pull you down into self-pity.

Joy in obedience

True obedience—
That comes when there is no doubt,
And you know there is no other way.
You recognize you are attached to a lifeline
And without it you will wither and shrivel up.
There is joy in true obedience
Because there is harmony:
One is in accord with all.

The Lord walks with me!

When in the world,
Think at all times: "The Lord walks with me!"
As though you were walking down the street
With the best-looking man or the most beautiful
    woman in the whole world!
Straighten up, hold your head high,
Smile a secret, happy smile,
And others will begin to meet me, see me,
Feel my light, serenity, and beauty
Shining out from you.

Wherever you are I am

Wherever you are I am,
And whatever you have to give
Is for where you are.
So don't wonder
What is going on over there.
Don't compare,
Don't feel that what you do depends on what
    people over there think.
Believe only in me
And in what I can do in you.
The greatest saints
Were modest, simple people
Who may have lived among others,
Yet were apart from them.
They were not unknown:
The earth knew of them;
All of nature and the angels in heaven gave thanks
For the light they brought to the earth.

Have you not stopped in a field,
Struck suddenly by the beauty of one particular
　　flower,
Be it alone or among others?
It spoke directly to you;
It gave you joy, gladness, comfort.
So may one be to others like that flower.

Gladness and acceptance

Stop worrying.
Stop straining to see and understand
Where you are to go,
What you are to do,
Why things are as they are.
You exhaust yourself doing that.
Get the right attitude of soul,
One of gladness and acceptance.
Gladness for all that is brought to you,
Acceptance of it all and of your very inability to
        understand God's plan.
This is not to say one shouldn't long to understand.
The longing and the acceptance
Are Hope and Faith,
Walking hand in hand,
One pulling forward,
The other looking around at where one is
With gladness.

One can never know enough about gladness and
    acceptance—
They are like plants within one
That must be allowed to grow.
Just because you think you know them already
Doesn't mean you don't greet them, think
    about them,
Get to know them a bit better.
Let your eyes be opened ever and again
To these seemingly simply little things
Which are the very cornerstones of life.

Be glad!

Be glad for all your uncertainties, your nervous
    spasms, your fears, your moments of loneliness;
Be glad, give thanks, praise the Lord!
When you give thanks, doors will be opened.
You will be able to see those dark, tight places in
    others,
You will be able to see where my light can pour in
And make whole.
You may even be able to will my light into others
From me, through you, on and on,
A holy weaving, a tapestry of love.
There will be sufferings
And temptations
To deepen you,
But always give thanks for them
And the fruits will be given to you.

Let your thoughts be continual "Thank yous" to
    Our Father.

True thanks

The deeper you can go into true thanks for what
   you have
The higher will you go in seeing and knowing what
   I would have you have.
If you focus on what you don't have
Then, truly, you have nothing.

Giving thanks

Giving thanks speeds up the "digestion" of daily
   life.
Most people aren't digesting life;
They're either choking on it, wallowing in it, or
   throwing it up.
Giving thanks provides the right "juices" for
   digestion to occur.

You may think you're giving thanks indiscrimi-
   nately for everything.
And in a sense you are,
But on another level your spirit is being quite
   discriminating.
It's taking in what it can use and letting what it
   can't use go by.
You can actually become conscious of this activity.
Persist in giving thanks
Even if you don't feel like it
And can see no earthly reason for it,

And the river of gladness and gratitude
Will find its way into and through you.

Give thanks also for others.
Give thanks for their infirmities, problems,
    grievances, even their lack of faith.
These thanks must, of course, come deep from
    your heart to be truly effective.

Gratitude is priceless.
It cannot be bought or sold.
It is the doorway into the spirit.
Too often you want to "get through" things.
To what?
Attempt to give thanks for where you are
    in this very moment.
It will help recollect you,
Open you to little things you're missing.
It will be food for those on the other side,

Many of whom suffer because they rushed
through their earthly lives.
When you do what they did not do,
It is balm for them.

What I wait for

Sometimes, when in doubt or suffering,
One must not ask and ask,
For I hear you,
I know your innermost thoughts and feelings.
What I wait for
Is a contrite heart,
The mind laid before me—
Your whole self there,
Waiting for my light,
Not for explanations
Or directions:
Just yourself made humble,
Willing to be glad
For all it endures.

Then will I gather you into myself.
Beyond words, you will know,
Beyond thoughts, you will believe,
Beyond feelings, you will love.

Lift

Lift your eyes to the spirit,
Don't plod along.

Keep your mind on me

Think not about the next thing you will do
When you are busy with what is at hand.
Keep your mind on me.
I am the Beginning and Ending of all,
And what happens to you in between
Depends on your holding me within.
Some never find the Beginning or the End—
The return home.
They wander and wander
Because they never knew their center.
I grieve for them;
They cannot pass through the fire without being
    burned.
They look out, not in.
Once you have found me within
You can find me outside—*everywhere!*
He who has ears to hear,
Let him hear.

I will fill you

You can get nowhere on your own strength.
You'll come to the end of it,
You'll go bankrupt,
You'll be but a dry, empty well.
If you can acknowledge this fact
And learn in your weakness to be silent,
I will fill you,
I will fill you to overflowing
With pure, sweet, life-giving water.

As it should be

Truly you do nothing
True and good
Of yourself:
Learn to wait,
Learn to listen,
Learn to be ever ready to do as I will—
And then act
So easily,
Almost without knowing you are acting
Or speaking my will.
Effortlessly!

That is as it should be.

Accept my help

You worry that you don't have enough self-
    control.
Of course you don't.
You never will.
That approach is hopeless—
Literally without hope.
Recognize how weak you are without me.
Don't get hung up on being too proud to accept
    my help—
That's what I'm here for.

Faith must be exercised

In your spirit body faith is as much a part of your
makeup
As bones and muscles are a part of your physical
body.
Like bones and muscles, faith must be fed,
exercised . . . *put into action.*
Otherwise the spirit body won't grow strong and
straight.
How do you feed faith?
How do you exercise it?
By asking daily for guidance
And acting on it.

Quietness

Learn quietness,
Earn quietness,
Await me
In quietness.
Hold your center
Still, expectant, ready,
Even in the confusion
Of outer life,
And I will speak.
Learn to listen this way
At all times,
Regardless of what I said a moment ago.

Quietness, quietness:
Let it expand within,
Making room
For the higher beings
In all their colors and forms
With all their divine music.

What does the human being on my path, the plain
   path, wear
But silence?

The new country

Can you bring your whole being to the frontier
    daily?
The frontier is inward, not outward.
It's waiting to be explored.

The spirit is often obscured by talk about spirit.
All the books, gadgets, odds and ends, and
    superstitions
People attach to themselves in the name of spirit—
One must be able to hack through that jungle.
The best weapon is the direct approach.
In fact, right now, it is the *only* weapon.

Each soul looking directly to me.
Each soul being ready and willing to leave all
    conceptions, all knowledge, all theories, all
    comfort behind.
Each soul being ready to listen for and stand up
    for me,

Regardless of what may happen to family, friends,
    financial security.
As this is done, so will the new country come into view.

Shed everything

In order to move on, to grow,
You must be willing to shed *everything*.
Even as you are shedding these words and
    messages—
Jotting them down, not looking back at them—
You recognize that you do not know anything,
You only sense the movement.
Later you will look back and see where you have
    been.

True courage

You are learning
What true courage is:
It is facing the unknown
With trust in me.
Think how the Vikings sailed off
Over the great ocean
With no idea where they were going,
What they might find,
Whether they would return or die.
Their courage protected them
And led them to land.
Yes, they had an idea, a longing
For what they hoped to find;
But first came the courage,
The leap into the unknown.

Courage is what I give you

When you have true faith in me.
Courage is the inner light
That burns, though all outside appears dark and
   threatening.
Courage silences the questioning mind,
The beating heart.

Strengthen your courage
By following it,
Believing in it,
Giving thanks for it.
It is I in you
Guiding you into the unknown.

Fear cuts you off

Fear cuts you off from me,
Cuts you off from your center, the source of all
    wisdom.
How many heart attacks could be avoided
If souls realized this!
Fear distorts your view of everything
Within and without.

The light within and the light without

In your work for me
The greater part of the burden lies in seeing,
And having to keep silence.
You are not to infringe
On any person's freedom.
How important is the inner work,
The inner working-out of things!
It is far more important than being able
To see angels, or elemental beings, or auras.
Let the light within
Strive to connect with the light without.
Learn to observe and honor this light in others,
Learn to speak only when you are told to speak;
Yet pray constantly.
For love never hesitates to come to the aid of
　　　the other,
No matter what you see, know, or think.

Love longs only for the good;
It never judges,
Is humble and modest in its bearing.

L o s e r s

If you praise God with your right hand,
Then mutter and grumble,
Your left hand is snatching back all that your
    right hand gave.

Likewise, if you pray earnestly for someone,
Then speak of that someone to everyone,
As though you, alone, know of the sufferings of
    that person,
Whatever light you have passed on to that person
    is diluted.
Your business is with me and that person
In the privacy of the inner room,
Not in the shopping mall!

Knowing nothing

Your strength lies in the fact that you know
    nothing,
And know you know nothing.
Then you are open, young at heart, unencumbered,
Free to do that which is poured through you.

Try to be glad all of today.
Glad for everything your eyes rest on,
For everything you can think of.

Silence and gladness

The greatest work is done in silence.
Not everyone who is chosen may speak:
There is a whole army that works silently
For the true freedom of all!
So must you attune yourself to me, and to me
    in others,
And be able to greet me silently,
And to obey every command without hesitation.
Don't compare and long for experiences such as
    others have;
Long only for my will,
For you do not know what I have in store for you!

Have the same awe and gladness
For the experiences of me that you sense in others,
Be they great or small, common or uncommon,
    pale or dazzling.
For through your gladness
You are helping others to be more open to me.

Never allow yourself to think, "I've heard of
    grander things that that" or
"I wish I could have that happen to me."
Encourage one another!
I cannot repeat this often enough!
As all flowers and plants grow together, facing
    sunwards in my garden,
No two experiences, no two lives will ever be alike.
And yet they are all One, are in the eternal, the
    Father.

God loves to paint!

You are the canvas on which God paints.
When you are open to me,
When you are full of praise,
When you make sacrifices on the physical level,
You are making more space on the canvas for God
    to paint.
How God loves to paint!
This doesn't mean you are a blank nothing.
On the contrary, you are most alive,
Most truly yourself,
When you are open to becoming picture after
    picture,
Daily, hourly.
To live within this stream of becoming
Is to live with God.

The physical world which you see with your physical
    eyes
Is not the whole world.

It is only the frame about the canvas.
Do not seek to be the only one
In the canvas God paints on.
Attempt to recognize how every life connected
    with yours
Is a part of this canvas too.

All children belong to God

The greatest single thing you can do for your
    children
Is to work upon yourself,
To make yourself a worthy vessel.

Remember, they are not really your children.
All children belong to God,
But he entrusts them to you.
And if you listen not to your expectations but to
    His,
He will guide you in your care of them.

You want so much to have the way all laid out.
Yet when you try to take hold of it,
It is all so vague in you
And your resolutions and projects do not always
    get very far.
How fortunate that is!

For children are ever growing and changing.
Their needs are changing:
What they need one day
May be quite different the next.
The same goes for what you see and personally
    like or dislike in them.
So ask daily and give thanks
That such a wonderful task has been given to you.

Of course you always have your special wishes for
    each one:
Trust in God, honesty, creativity, joy in life.
Maybe, unknowingly, they have given these wishes
    to you,
As though entrusting you with precious jewels,
That you may look after and protect the very
    qualities they themselves hope to take on
    some day.

Haven't you observed how your wishes for each
    child differ?

Trust these wishes,
And be large enough to hope for those qualities
    within yourself too.
Does not love propagate spiritually as well as
    physically?
And is it not just that your two bodies have created
    theirs
But that they, in their coming, can create *you* each
    anew?

Even as characteristics are handed down
From one generation to the next
And you become conscious of them,
So may the noble thought, "I shall transform this
    quality in myself" also be handed down—

As long as you do not allow pride in them, in yourself, or in what you see of yourself in them
To blind you in any way.

Children are like flowers

Your children are like flowers.

You are their sun.

Give warmth and cheerfulness and they will grow
straight and strong.

Do not comment on their differences, or your
preferences;

Be glad for whatever grows in your garden.

The future in the young

Love the future that you sense in the young.
Do not fear it, or criticize the strange forms it
   may take.
Do not doubt that the highest in them
Will be able to handle its apparently strange
   manifestations.
Nourish the future in them,
For they, too, move on the stream of becoming.

Care for the body

The physical world must be loved and honored as
the house of the spirit world.
Therefore cherish and care for you body
And the bodies of your children.
The body is the temple wherein I dwell.
Should you neglect or harm it in any way,
I, too, am crippled and made less.

The age of the spirit within you and the age of
your physical body do not always correspond.
In fact, they rarely correspond.
A little child may have within it an old wise spirit;
An old body may have within it a young,
unformed spirit.
A wise spirit is never hardened within itself.
A wise spirit is flexible, soft, trusting,
It is as a child.

Guardian Angels

Every child has a being who watches over her, guides
her, shapes her in the early years
And remains near through the life of that soul
    on earth.
Some call this being the Guardian Angel.
Those who love rightly work and converse with
    these beings.
Listen carefully for thoughts from the Guardian
    Angels,
For when you listen to them
You are listening to God.
The Guardian Angels are an extension of God.

There are spirits that watch over the plants and
    the animals.
There is nothing vague or nebulous about them.
Imagine the animals belonging to clubs:
The Dog Club, the Bird Club, the Butterfly Club.
If you have known and truly loved one dog, one
    bird, or one butterfly
You have entered into the spirit of that club.
You have inwardly connected with the spirit of dog,
    bird, or butterfly.
You *can* become conscious of this.
The spirits await your awakening to them.
The plants also belong to clubs—
Moss, marigold, pea, pine—
Each has its distinct characteristics,
Each is holy and beautiful,
Each is of The Word.

You too must die

Look upon the decaying and dying plants.
You, too, must die if you are to rise.
Even death is beautiful.

Within every true love I am

Behind every action and thought there is a living
    reality.
Desire and sex are not things one must "overcome,"
They are colors on the palette,
No picture would be complete without them.
As you desire, and as pleasure and release come to
    you in the act of sex,
Sense how I desire fusion with you.
Ideals are born in this fusion.
Thus there is a kind of "sex" in the spiritual world
    also.

Those who are fearful of sex are fearful of the whole.
Know that sex for its own sake only is a dead end,
But sex as a part of love must not be ignored,
For it helps to show you your incompleteness, it
    stirs in you the longing to create.

Imagine the masculine and femine bodies as the
    two parts of a shell that fit together to
    become one whole.
Imagine day and night and how they become
    one whole.
Within every soul are both, masculine and
feminine, day and night.
Within every true bond is the third—
This is a great mystery:
Within every true love, I am.

Acknowledge your feelings

You cannot deny your feelings,
Even as you cannot deny
The existence of the physical world around you.
Your soul life with its feelings,
Provides the ore
Which the spirit can forge into metal:
Metal for tools,
Metal for weapons,
Metal for building.
Acknowledge your feelings;
Bring them up to the light.

I am here to help

Most of the time you cannot see where
The feelings and thoughts that arise within you
    come from—
So forcefully, so suddenly!
You feel like a blade of grass
Bent over backwards by the wind,
Whipped this way and that.
Do not allow these feelings and thoughts to
    break you.
You still them,
You *can* transform them,
Ask—
I am here to help.

Love never compels

I cannot compel you to come to me,
Or to do this or that.
Love never compels.
When you think, "I must do this . . ." yet you
    hesitate, or cannot do it,
And then feel guilty afterwards,
It is because there is no love in your thoughts,
You are thinking of me as duty, as burden and
    obligation.

Through your conscience I may suggest something,
And if you know, "This is the right thing for me
    to do,"
You will realize it is always for your own good,
Not for my gain.
Love longs for what is good
To come into being in you,
As the gardener longs for his flowers
To grow into their true splendor.

Rightly received,
A message from love
Will kindle love in you—
Love to do the deed.

Who is it that loves?

You say, "I love . . ."
You feel love welling up within for your family
   and your friends.
Sometimes you are bewildered by the love you
   feel for others,
You even wonder if it is right.
But *who* is it that loves?

I AM LOVE.
It is I in you, I loving *through* you!
Remember this: love is a gift,
So honor and cherish it,
And accept it with wonder.
Do not allow your mind to manipulate it,
Do not allow your feelings to seize hold of and
   possess it,
For then it will become like stale water.
You can never own love,
You can only let love own you.

Let love flow, let it take you where it will;
You will know what is right and wrong.
You will not fret when it seems to disappear
    altogether—
It has only gone underground.
When you truly love another,
That love is forever
Though, in every outer way, you may appear to
    have moved on.
When you truly love
You are within the other, the other is within you,
Together you are in me.

When you do not hug the love that is given to you
But allow it to become true gladness for life,
There can be no barrier
Between you and anyone else.
For when love shines out from you into all,

Like a light that cannot be quenched,
Others are drawn to you,
Even in spite of yourself.
Like moths drawn to a flame,
They seek what they do not have;
They long for the light in themselves,
And as light can enter in through even the tiniest
        crack,
Even so, they begin to open.

To love means to open one's self
To my holy stream,
That it may flow within: from the Father,
Through me, through you, out into the world.

Let me love you!

Dear sweet, impatient soul,
Don't strain to prove yourself,
Just let me love you!

Love knows the other

I do not want just your joy, your raptures
At my presence—
Do you, as you are loved, want not only
The warmth of affection
But also the clarity of Love's intelligence?
For Love *knows* the other,
Knows his coming and goings,
His complete and incomplete moments.
True Love longs to help make the other complete
As God, our Father, would have us be.
So seek to know me, not only as warmth but as
    light,
Light that sees,
And in seeing hears,
And in hearing knows,
And in knowing wills
That Our Father's will may be complete.

Feel this in your heart

Attempt to feel this in your heart: *I love all human beings!*

Regardless of their weaknesses and sins.

Love calls to love

If you truly long to know me in every way
Then look for me
In everyone and everything you see.

I am in every person
Though that person may not know it,
Though I may be buried deep.
But look for me in every person
And help me to be seen.
Only love can see me
And can help me to come forth and shine.
For I am love
Love calls to love.

That which is most true

I am that which is most true in each person.
I am that which each person longs for most
Though he or she may not know it.

One with Him

Every person longs to be loved
For himself, as himself.
He longs to feel he is the first and the last,
The one and only,
And that he is forgiven this longing,
Selfish as it may seem.
Perhaps God, your Father, gave you this very
    longing
When He fashioned you.
That you might seek and seek for Him
And finally find yourself to be one with Him,
Made complete in His love.

Who truly loves

He who truly loves
Rests with no person
For he follows after
The Master of Love.

And lo, behold, he finds,
As he goes on,
All whom he loves are there
Within him!

Deepen yourself for love

Do not allow your mind to try to determine what
    I am going to say.
This does happen.
Do not allow your mind to grab hold of details,
Thus missing the larger spirit of what I'm saying.
If you are truly open to what I'm saying, you will
    act on it without questioning the why, where,
    or how.
There will be no room for judgment or fussing of
    any kind.
Every day is important
Yet what you consider a long time is nothing.
Two years, ten years, twenty years of listening are
    nothing
Beside the joy and certainty one can know at the
    end of that time.
Seek ever to deepen yourself in every way for love.

To love is to listen

To love is to listen.
Thus the First Commandment means to listen to
the Lord in every way.
And the Second Commandment means to listen
to all people.

The ear of ears is in the heart

To listen means to open your heart to another.
The heart is not just pure feeling, gushing emo-
tion, sentimentality.
It is in the heart that the true thought can be
heard.
The ear of ears is in the heart.

Let the water be ever fresh

Be like the river banks:
They hold the waters
And are shaped by them,
But they cannot make the waters
Go this way
Or that way;
Nor can they keep the waters.
Their joy is in being the passageway.
The water would turn foul,
Were it not allowed to move on.
And while the water is ever water,
And therefore ever the same,
It is also ever different,
Ever fresh.

Humility

True humility is dependence on God.
Sometimes the one who makes himself out to be
    most humble
Is, in reality, most proud.
To be truly humble
Is to know God is your creator
And never to lose sight of that
No matter what you have done
Or what people think of you,
For you will count the honor from others
As nothing beside the honor from God.
God does honor us,
And great are His love and joy
When we recognize this and yield our hearts to Him.

To be humble does not mean to belittle yourself.
Indeed, one may have to step forward, take
    responsibility,

And be a leader.
When one is open to me,
One may have to stand up and stick out.

The eternal behind all things

As I am in you
So will you learn to see me outside.
The more I am in you
The more will you see,
Until what you see
Ceases to surprise you—
Delights
But does not frighten you.
You will see the eternal
Behind all things:
The Word that created that thing,
And exactly how it was meant to be.
Truth changes as it grows,
Yet the beginning, the seed, is always there.
The seer can see this seed
And all the forms and variations of its growth,
Whereas you see the plant only in it present form.
Here is a task: Try to see each living thing
In its many stages, that eventually you may
        recognize the Word.

Behind everything physical there is the spiritual:
Absorb that!
Yes, behind everything man-made
There is the spiritual,
Though it is harder to discern;
And man, in his material inflexibility,
May have created something inflexible;
But nevertheless that thing has a spiritual origin.

Be filled with the thought of all that is spiritual,
Of all that seeks to be born on the physical plane.
Be filled with the thought that
All around one in the physical, material world
The spirit longs to go on growing and evolving,
Though that growth is too subtle for human eyes.
Ask for the spiritual eyes
To see these things,
That you may help them in every way

And not hinder them with your blindness and
  smallness.

No one is a true seer
Unless he gives up all desire to see.

Don't rush, don't strain

Don't rush.
Don't strain your senses
To do what they are not yet meant to do.
You *must* be firmly grounded.
Otherwise you will make yourself ill
And harm others.

Take heart, believe

All work with me is an adventure, a coming into
    being, a becoming.
You may see nothing outwardly,
And that may discourage you at times;
But take heart, believe in me,
Know that the work being done in the invisible
    realms
Is more grand than anything you can imagine
    just now.
Some day you will see it, you will live right into it,
You will feel, "This is what I dreamt and, indeed, it
    is true!"

Open your imagination to me

Do not worry that you are imagining everything.
Open your imagination to me.
In your imagining you are hoping for the spirit,
    believing in it, preparing for it.
Your imagination,
Which is really only a tiny crack admitting a shaft
    of my light,
Most be opened more and more for me—
The Truth, the True Reality.
It will be even more splendid
Than the little shaft of light you see now.
Above all it will be whole and complete in a way
You do not know.
You will learn with time to distinguish
Between what is true, healthy imagining,
And what is mere fantasy and day-dreaming.
One can be as clear as the day it calls forth
    strength in you, strength to act, and it fills
    you with gladness.

The other sticks to you like fly-paper, lulls you into inactivity.

Imagination and intuition

You don't have imagination.
Opening your inner senses to me, seeing the world
    through me—
What you then see is what you call imagination.
Intuition is opening your spirit to me.

Come to meet me

If you long to see me,
Then you must come to meet me.
It is not a matter of my hiding myself from you
So much as it is that your sight is still veiled.
This is a protection in itself:
Just as the seed is covered by a coat
And only after its roots have gone down a good way,
And it has pushed up through the coat and through
    the earth,
Is it truly fit to see the sun.
The seed knows which way to grow
To meet the sun—
So it is that it "sees" the sun
Before actually coming into contact with it.
Trust this instinct,
This movement through darkness and uncertainity
    towards me.
Do not rush it,
For the roots must be very strong and secure.

Give up your ideas about "work"

You say you want work?
I have plenty of work for you to do!
Here goes:
Give up your outer ideas about "work,"
Learn to be comfortable with me in every way,
Enjoy everything you do,
Take walks and tell me about them,
See people and tell me how they are,
Laugh when you're confused,
Cry when you're happy.

Give, and give, and give to me,
And I will give to you in great abundance.
This giving and receiving will be your "work"—
And your "play"!

Let your actions be prayers.

Say   yes   to   what   I   bring   you

You cannot be my worker
If you can't keep your eye on me.
This means saying no
To all kinds of distractions
And yes to whatever I bring you,
No matter how unconnected or irrelevant it seems
Beside what you are presently doing.
Don't I know the business
Better than you?
Can't I see farther than you?
Haven't I been in it quite a bit longer than you?

Trust me.
Be my worker
Cheerfully, willingly.

My workers must have firm roots

Do not chat about "spiritual matters."
Keep your intuitions to yourself,
Unless it's clear they will be helpful.
Think first of loving all,
Thus listening to all.
Let no dark thoughts interfere,
That the soul within each may speak.
Do your work, even the smallest chores gladly.
My workers must have firm roots in the earth.

Step back into the silence

When people confront you with questions
Or bring you their problems,
Step back into the silence.
You will find the answers there.
Always step back into the silence!

Spirit greets spirit in the silence

You must be strong in the spirit world,
Rooted firmly in it,
If you are to be my helper in the physical world.
In true Christ consciousness
There is no room for self-consciousness.
This is one way you can learn to measure yourself,
To see how completely you have given yourself to
    me.

Look all about for the spirit world: in nature, in
    children, in other people, in the Book.
Greet it!
The spirit in you will be strengthened,
And in others, and in nature also.
Spirit greets spirit in the silence.

Keep life simple and direct

You mistrust me and what you hear when you
    think,
"Maybe I need to do exercises."
You are like the woman continually over-stocking
    her pantry,
Not going by the needs of the moment.
I can tell you of plenty of exercises!
Some of them will make you laugh and wonder if
you are doing anything "worthwhile."
Just listen!—that's the first and only real exercise.
Through your listening keep life simple and direct.

Learn to be matter-of-fact—
NOW!

Listen for true need

Learn to listen yet more deeply for the true
    needs of others.
I do not give anything unless there is a true
    need.

Open the way

When you can put aside every negative thought,
Opening the way
To being connected with me,
Your whole day will take on order and meaning.
Harmony will prevail,
Not only within you,
But all around you.

Look first for the good

What is it to worry,
But to rush round and round in circles
Over one thing?
What a help that is!
To be truly helpful
Requires a certain detachment,
The ability to see things as they are
And can be.
Seeing what they can be
Helps to draw it out of them.
So always look first for the good in a situation;
Then you will begin to see what it may become.

The effort matters

It is the effort that matters,
Not the result.
The quality of the effort:
Did you give ALL
Or where you half-hearted?
Did you keep your eye on me
And not allow yourself to be the least bit
 distracted by outer circumstances?

Never assume anything with me

You must never assume anything with me.
That I am near, that I love you and will guide
    you—
You must have *faith* in that.
But to assume I am near,
To assume I love you and will guide you,
To assume I want you to do this or that,
Without consulting me,
That's allowing things to go slack.
Feel the difference between assuming I'm near,
And turning to me daily.

As you go upwards

Of course things become more perilous
As you go upwards!
How else would they be?
The cliffs are more jagged
Yet the view is more and more grand.
Be glad!

Selfishness exhausts

If you truly live in me
You will never be exhausted.
The more you open yourself to love,
The more love can create through you.
Selfishness exhausts you,
Eats you up,
Burns you out.
Selfishness is ingratitude
Spiraling downwards into darkness.
Whenever you feel exhausted,
Stop.
Step back,
Seek out the underlying attitude:
Are you doing this for yourself, or for me?
Then give thanks.

Hearts must come to me

There are many who work with my love in their hearts.
They mean well, they do well, they give selflessly
    of themselves
For the good of the world.
They are content and happy
Without having, or asking for, a glimse into the higher.
They are like an army
Marching slowly but surely onwards.

Now, in the times to come, all must look for the
    higher.
Every soul must move onwards with the same sure
    faith,
But it must dare to believe it *can* see, hear and meet
That which calls to it.
This meeting will create the Second Coming.
I, alone, do not come to humanity,
The hearts of all must come to me.

The Father knows

The Father knows the most vulnerable spot in
    every heart.
He will not hesitate to touch it
If pain will bring that soul to Him.

Doors to the spirit

Pain and sorrow are doors to the spirit,
As are joy and gratitude.
Most people try to distance themselves from pain
    and sorrow,
Rather than going through them.

"Lord, be in me!"

Pain cleanses and purifies.
If you are in pain,
Know that you need to be cleansed.
Submit willingly to be cleansed.

And those times when you feel sick in your soul,
When you are paralyzed by a sadness you cannot
    see, or touch, or find the right ointment for,
Ask over and over, "Lord, be in me!"
Let that thought become your very breath.
For it may be that something in you is trying to
    reach me,
But something else will not allow it.
"Lord, be in me! Lord, be in me!" That can wear
    away mountains of resistance, if said rightly
    from your very heart.

True relaxation

There is a paradox in the truth that you can do real w
only if you are relaxed.
You must be resting in my love and the knowledge
of Our Father's wisdom.
True relaxation never implies laziness or sleepiness.
It is a state of vibrant awareness.

When confused

When you are confused
Don't toss about and look without for answers.
Acknowledge the confusion and bid it go from you.
Then go about your daily tasks.
Hold yourself straight in patience and calmness,
Trusting that the connection between us will be
revealed again.

When in distress

If you cannot give up all to me when in distress,
Combat the confused thoughts and feelings by
    taking another thought or feeling
And placing it in the center of your being.
Turn your inner eye on it
That it may swell and grow and take form
    within you.

Have patience

If you could understand now why you are
    suffering
You wouldn't be suffering.
That's a fact.
Since you can't understand now,
Have patience.

As I've said elsewhere,
"In patience possess ye your soul."
What does that mean?
It means having perfect faith.
It means keeping on,
Though you see nothing
And the darkness seems absolute.
Patience will lead you to understanding.

A great waiting

I waited so long for you to come to me.
And still I wait for you—ALL of you.
Love is a great waiting, a great patience.
Why, then, can you not wait for me?

Only . . .

Only when you are most low
Can you receive the highest,
Only when you are most empty
Can you be filled,
Only when you are truly at rest
Can Christ be active in you.

Helping others

When you take the work of someone else upon
　　yourself,
Something is taken from you.
Don't take on unnecessary burdens,
Don't barge into other people's lives,
Don't meddle with God's plans.
If it is God's plan for you to help another, you will
　　be told.
Trust that.
The best you can do, in the meantime,
Is to hold yourself empty.
When you are given a task, the strength will be
　　given to you.
You will be able to accomplish things you never
　　realized you could do.

The other side of sorrow

The other side of sorrow
Is joy.
When you can raise your sorrow up
Above bitterness, above disappointment,
    above pain,
To the light—
A birth occurs.
In heaven the angels rejoice.
Those who have died are fed.
On earth the very soil is made new.

You must help one another unceasingly to find
    the light.
This is why you must love your neighbor as
    yourself.
God, the Father, longs to give you joy
As he takes your sorrows.
The earth can pass away when all can do this.
A new world will begin.

This is all more wonderful
Than anything you can imagine.

Right wishing

How terribly people want certain things,
Believing these things are right for themselves or
    for others.
Only Our Father knows what is truly right for us,
Yet many people get what they want
Out of the very force of their wanting
And wrong wishing.

Imagine the patience of the Father
Waiting for them to wish as He wishes—
Of their own free will.
And how is one to know what is right wishing?
Through this: through the inflow of strength and
    love
That makes all work easy, effortless, truly joyful.
Remember: one cannot find this once and for all;
One must win it anew
Daily.

The goal

Wisdom translated into will,
Into action, into creation:
That is the highest goal.
That *is* the goal.

Your will must be welded

Your will—that which moves so forcefully in your
lower self and often with good intention—
Must be welded to your higher self,
If you want your actions to have meaning in a
    spiritual way.
Otherwise all activity is mere "busy-ness" and
motion undirected, and in the end worth little.

The way to health

There is such sickness in the souls of men and
     women!
The root of this sickness is the need to be united
     with the true source, with the divine.
The sooner souls recognize this need and turn
     to me,
The sooner will they find true health.

Send transfusions of love

Send transfusions of love to others,
Silently in your prayers.
Be blind to all outer signs of illness and darkness
As you send light to them.

Legions of angels

Just as you pray for others,
Know that others
Whom you cannot see
Pray for you.
Be humbled by that.
There is so little you can accomplish by yourself.
And do not ever think
You alone pray for another.
There are legions of angels working for me,
As well as spirits on earth and above.
Know that this work is an act of pure love
Binding many together,
Spreading light, music, joy,
Opposing the dark forces that alienate and harden
 man in himself.
This is love in its glory,
In its endless interweaving.

Man's capacities to love and to pray are so small;
But can be so grand,
If he be humbled in the knowledge
Of how little he does and can do himself.
It is a matter of opening one's self,
Of becoming an instrument on which Love can
    play.

Being chosen

Many are called, few are chosen.
Many feel the call,
But few know what the call requires.
You must answer daily to this call,
Even minutely,
If you would be chosen.
Being chosen means
Choosing out of your own will
To do God's will.

Be

Be what you believe!

Servant to all

Who is greater: the master or the servant?
Each has a place, each has work, each is a part of
    the whole.
The whole would be incomplete without either.
Learn to be master of yourself
And servant to all.

When you feel homesick

Imagine you're a traveler from another country.
You have not been home for a long time
But you know you will return home some time
    again.
When you feel homesick
Look for beautiful things all around to call home
    about—
That will bring home closer.

A channel of my love

Pray only to be a channel of my love into others—
Silently.

Know that you need not know about others
In order to pray my light into them.

Think the best

You simply can't see everything.
Therefore,
Think well of others,
No matter what people say about them.
Think the best
No matter how difficult the situation appears to be.

Look for the light in others

You worry about being judgmental—
Rouse yourself again and again to look for the light
 in others.
When you're looking for it
There is no room in you for critical thoughts.

Soon you'll realize you simply can't love a person
 less
Because his or her path is longer.
In fact, you'll find yourself loving that person more.

When you forgive

When you forgive another
You are giving that person the power to do the
   right thing.
It is the same when you forgive yourself.
When you withhold forgiveness
You are withholding the power.
Do you really want that?

Guilt and forgiveness

Guilt can kill all longing for me.
Every soul senses the eternal within itself.
It also senses how it is pulled down again and
    again
By the earthly.
That it has given in again and again to the earthly
Can arouse such guilt.

The important thing is to be able to say,
"I gave in and it led nowhere—forgive me."
The moment you can say that
You are with me again.
Never let your heart forget this.

Only forgiveness

There is no excuse for not acting from your highest.
Don't say, "I am only human..."
There is only forgiveness—
The sooner you ask for it and move on,
The better.

Only God

No human being is ever fully right
Or completely wrong.
Only God, the Father, is fully and completely right.

You can find true forgiveness in me

Be glad for feeling out of touch,
For recognizing your need for forgiveness.
Through gladness you can return to me instantly.
You can find true forgiveness in me
Wherever you are,
However it is with you.
This forgiveness does not scold and threaten,
It does not hold up pictures
Reminding you of what you've done.
It offers a new beginning.
It gives your true self back to you
No matter what the deed.
Its trademark is joy—
My joy because you have returned freely to me.
Yes, I want you to be free,
Free to wander,
And return.

I know you through and through!

I know you through and through!

Once you know me personally,
You are not afraid of anything impersonal entering
  into our relationship.
You can reach out and touch the personal in every
  human being.
You long for every soul to know me in their very
  own personal way.

Put your hope in me

Do not put your hope in any person.
If you do, you will be disappointed.
Put your hope in me
And you will never know disappointment.
Having done this,
You will learn to listen for the spirit that speaks
    through every person
And seeks expression.
You will be helping to give expression to the spirit.

I come first

You are forgetting that I come first,
Not all these people you want to help.
In your eagerness you're losing sight of me.
I will not be crowded
Out of my own house!
I will permit illness to enter
If that is the only way
I can remind you that *I* come first.

Once you understand this you will be able to look
    upon suffering
As from a distance, without becoming entangled
    in it.
You will remember to come to me for help,
To ask in my name,
Never from your own name, or your own resources.

You will learn to rise up to the light,
Not slip down in the darkness.

You will learn how the whole world
Awaits this rising of humanity
Above the dark forces
That would pull it down.
You will learn to recognize
When a misfortune is a gift,
A message from me,
And when it is a manifestation
Of a dark force.

Responsibilities

Seeing and hearing are responsibilities.
As you see and hear into the spiritual world
You become a citizen of that world.
You learn its rules:
You don't get something for nothing.

Time can do wonders

If you do not hear right away
When in a difficult situation
And are unable to see the positive in it,
Command your mind to be silent and empty,
Utterly empty.
Forbid your mind
To jump for the nearest thought,
Like a dog desperate for a bone to gnaw.
Time can do wonders.
Time can bring your heart the perspective you
     need.
True, there is no time at the center,
Wherein is eternity.
But outside the center
Time, like an elastic,
Holds you together,
Draws you slowly inwards.

Wisdom and action

Most people reap wisdom at the end of their lives.
It comes to them, comes before them,
Is carried on with them into their next life.
Thus they learn through their actions.

To give wisdom form through action,
Will be the task of man
In times to come.
One can begin by opening oneself to the higher
    thoughts,
Conversing with them,
Becoming familar with them,
Letting them dwell and grow within.

Truth

Truth can be simple, nourishing bread
Or it can be fancy cake—
Depending on how you take it.

Yours or mine?

When you think you are giving form to a thought
Are you making it yours, or mine?
There is a huge difference between the two.

Nourish a thought

You must learn to say "No" to some thoughts and
    feelings
No matter how beautiful and wonderful they seem,
That certain thoughts can truly take root in you
And grow outwards into actions that bear fruit,
    fruit of my vine.

How can you know which thoughts these are?
Do not worry,
You will know with an inner certainty
When those thoughts draw near.
Trust this knowing.

The thoughts you say "Yes" to
Will think themselves into and out of you.
There are laws to the way in which such thoughts
arise, come, grow, blossom, die back
within themselves and are born again.
You will be yielding yourself to these laws.

Gradually they will reveal themselves to your
    consciousness.
But first, do not worry,
Trust the knowing in your heart.
Then learn to nourish a thought all the way
    through.

Go out now and open yourself to Divine Order
    and Harmony.

Let thoughts live

Take thoughts and let them live within you.
Let them show you their selves
Without your grasping hold of them.
Let them speak to you in their different forms,
So that they might let you clothe them in actions.

Know that a thought may wear many different
    clothes.
Don't let this dismay you;
Rather be humbled by the manifold ways of
    thoughts,
Be humbled by your own smallness beside them.
Even Satan is a thought
Capable of wearing many different disguises.
If you are secure in the thought of me, your Christ,
    your light and strength,
You will be able to view all thoughts safely
And will come to know them for their true worth.

Heed the seasons

Heed the seasons,
Heed nature;
Nature has the key to the festivals on earth.
The festivals in heaven
Are of another kind.
Some day all of humanity will be invited to
    participate in them.

Advent verse

I was here in worlds
Before you were here.
I came again
When you were young,
That you might know
The tenderness of the young.
Then, when all was hardening within you,
I gave myself
That you might ever be open
To the weaving, turning and spinning
Of the heavenly spheres.

The flowers, trees, birds, stones:
They know all this;
It is a part of their being.
They would speak of it all to you
If you would but pause and listen.
So let your sole wish be
To be open—

As flowers are open,
As birds are whole in the openness of flight,
As rocks await their breaking, their opening
To light.

Renewal at Christmas

The soul's longing and hope for truth
Are now renewed.
New strength and love for truth
Are given to it.
Having sunk down into the depth and darkness
    of its being
The soul turns its eyes heavenwards again.

So also are the animals and plants quickened,
And given renewed faith.
Every plant is now given
That force anew—to praise, to grow.
Yes, even plants know what it is to praise God.
Through their growing and unfolding
They give thanks.

Unto each human soul is given the love of the
    spiritual.
Through that love all outer deeds will flow.

All actions, all creations,
All that is true and good
Will come into being.
During these days be still, glad, and quietly joyful
For all that is given to you and yours.
Pray that it be lovingly received.
Pray that it be directed rightly
Heavenwards.

Rest in me

What does it mean to "Rest in me?"

It means I am not only
In the house, room, or garden
You create within in your prayers.
It means I am without, too:
In the air you breathe,
The earth you walk on,
The stars you look up at.
If you can feel me outwardly as well as inwardly,
You will become like a swimmer
Floating on your back,
Looking skywards,
Moving your body only the smallest bit—
Relaxing in me, the ocean.

You will learn,
By trusting me,

To ride every wave,
No matter how large and threatening.
You will learn to hear
Every current of my *Be*-ing.

Can you do it?
Can you learn to rest in me
At all times?
Even as you breathe in the air
And breathe it out—
As long as you live on the earth.

Rest in the air—
Which is invisible
Yet all-sustaining—
Taking what you need,
Giving back what you don't need,
No more, no less.

To rest in me
Is to give up all to me,
To know that I will give you
All that is right and necessary.
Hear the perfect breathing therein:
I give to you,
You give to me;
Out of this we *both* grow,

To rest in me
Is to live in perfect praise.

Strung together

Look at that necklace there—
All of the beads are beautiful,
Each one is a world, a sphere within itself.
See how the light reflects and shines in each one.
Cover one bead and there is a gap,
The rhythm of the whole is lost.
Pull one bead out by force
And the whole is broken . . . scattered.
Learn from this necklace
How every thought, every action
Done for my sake
Is beautiful and complete in itself;
All part of a whole,
All strung together by love.

Let no weary thought,
No discouragement or fear
Ever tug at the love
That holds you to me.

Spin on, dear heart

Know that you can spin golden thoughts of love
    heavenwards
To Our Father.
Know as you spin
That heaven is your true home,
But do not be anxious or overeager to return there.
Know that this spinning
Is what you are here on earth for:
To spin heavenwards and outwards
Into the divine in all people,
To feel the glorious tapestry of love
Growing stronger, wider, and deeper every day.
See it inwardly!
Never leave off spinning.
Though some places appear finished,
They are never "finished,"
They can become yet more beautiful.
Though some places appear thin, worn, and ready
    to break,

Though some places seem to reject your gift and
    send out dark threads,
Spin on, dear heart, spin on!

The wiser, the quieter

The wiser one is
The quieter one is,
For the truly wise one knows
He knows nothing
Except that he must listen,
And through listening
Learn to speak and act.

The spirit moves

How you feel,
Or how things seem,
The spirit moves deep within.
Keep still and listen.

The I AM is forever

Turn your eye inwards,
Reach all the way to stillness,
Darkness, silence,
To the point where
In-breath and out-breath meet.
Meet your I.
Let the recognition rise up:

I AM.

Let it grow slowly, surely, steadily:

I AM light,
I AM love,
I AM goodness, truth and beauty.

There should be nothing forced about this.
If the I am is true

You will feel light, love, goodness, truth and beauty
Rising up in you,
Interweaving.
You will know they are you,
And, beyond that, you will know
No matter how small, weak and imperfect your body,
You ARE.

You, as light, love, goodness, truth and beauty, will
        go on, and on, and on.
Fear will fall away.

If you cannot fill
The form your body thinks it must fill
That is all right.
There will be another time.

The I AM is forever.